JUL 01

Everything
You Need to
Know About

The
Dangers
of Sports
Gambling

Teen gambling, including betting on sports, has risen steadily in recent years.

Everything
You Need to
Know About

The Dangers of Sports Gambling

Joshua D. G. Willker

The Rosen Publishing Group, Inc.
New York

Published in 2000 by The Rosen Publishing Group, Inc.
29 East 21st Street, New York, NY 10010

First Edition

Library of Congress Cataloging-in-Publication Data

Wilker, Josh.
    Everything you need to know about sports gambling / Joshua Wilker.— 1st ed.
       p. cm.— (The need to know library)
    ISBN 0-8239-3229-X
    1. Sports betting. 2. Compulsive Gambling. I. Title. II. Series.
GV717 .W53 2000
796—dc21   00-009098

Manufactured in the United States of America

Contents

Chapter One | It's Not Whether You Win or Lose

Although not everyone involved agreed that it was absolutely the best postseason game they had ever played in or watched, there was no question about one thing: It was the longest. When, on the night of Sunday, October 17, 1999, the fifth game of the National League Championship series came to an end, it had lasted fifteen innings—a total of five hours and forty-seven minutes. In terms of time, that made it the longest postseason game in the history of Major League Baseball.

The contestants that night were the Atlanta Braves and the New York Mets. The Braves were a perennial powerhouse, winners of their division of the National League every year of the 1990s.

The Mets celebrate their victory over the Braves in Game Five of the 1999 National League Championship series.

Their challengers, the Mets, were upstarts who had risen from the bottom of the league's standings to challenge Atlanta.

Early on in the series, the underdog Mets appeared overwhelmed by the mighty Braves, who won the first three games of the best-of-seven series. But down by a run in the bottom of the eighth inning in Game Four, just five outs from elimination, the Mets showed the heart and resiliency that had served them so well all year. They scratched together two runs and held on in the ninth for the win.

Fans agreed that the game had been a classic, with a little bit of everything that makes the postseason so exciting for players and fans alike—sterling pitching, clutch hitting, spectacular fielding, and a duel of wits between the opposing managers, Atlanta's low-key Bobby Cox and New York's preening Bobby Valentine.

As good as Game Four had been, it only set the stage for Game Five. The game was fraught with tension from the outset. Atlanta took the early lead, but the Mets battled back. Still, they found themselves trailing as they went into their final at-bat in the bottom of the ninth. Would it be their last ups of the season?

Not yet. A walk, a sacrifice bunt, and a single from a seldom-used reserve enabled the plucky Mets to tie the score at two, and the game went into extra innings.

Extra innings quickly became a chess match between the two managers, a whirlwind of strategic moves, including pitching changes, pinch hitters, defensive replacements, pinch runners, and double switches. By the time the game ended, the two teams would set a record for the number of players—forty-five—that they used.

Tension mounted as the innings stretched on, and neither team was able to break through. Finally, in the top of the fifteenth inning, the Braves pushed across a run against the Mets' last pitcher, the fireballing rookie Octavio Dotel.

Down to their last gasp once more, the Mets mustered one last, improbable rally. Seemingly unnerved by the pressure, with more than 50,000 leather-lunged New Yorkers screaming at him, the Braves' own rookie reliever, Kevin McGlinchy, began experiencing control problems. The Mets loaded the bases. Still unable to find the plate, McGlinchy walked the Mets' last reserve, pinch hitter and back-up catcher Todd Pratt, to force in a run and tie the game once again, this time at three runs apiece.

Up to the plate stepped Robin Ventura. It was a situation that probably every young baseball fan has played out in his dreams at some point: The most important game of the season, game tied, the home team's last at-bat, bases loaded, fans roaring, and you step up to the plate, able to settle matters with just one swing.

And then Ventura lived out the fantasy, picking on a fat pitch from McGlinchy and scorching a low line drive to right field. Deep to right field. Very deep. As 50,000 fans at the stadium and millions of television viewers screamed in disbelief and delirium, the ball carried over the outfield wall for a game-winning grand-slam home run.

On the field, as the Braves trudged sadly off to their clubhouse, the Mets reacted as if they were

9

Robin Ventura hit a game-winning grand-slam home run in the 1999 National League Championships.

in shock. As the runner from third crossed home plate with the winning run, the two runners behind him temporarily lost their bearings. Joy outweighed the professional ballplayers' unwritten code of conduct for such situations, and the two Mets who were between bases began leaping into the air in celebration. Then they turned back, journeying the wrong way around the base paths and interrupting Ventura's triumphant home-run trot. Somewhere around second base, an impromptu celebratory melee took place, with the ecstatic Mets piling onto Ventura and one another. Confetti and cheers rained down from the stands. Neither Ventura nor the other two runners ever reached home plate.

In the joy of the moment, that fact seemed of little importance. The runner on third had been clearheaded enough to actually touch home plate before celebrating, which meant his run counted. And his was the only one that counted. So officially, in accordance with baseball's time-honored rules, the final score was only 4 to 3 in favor of the Mets. Ventura was credited with only a single instead of a home run, with just one run batted in instead of four.

For Ventura and the other players, it hardly mattered. The result that counted—which team won the game—was unchanged. For those who follow sports for the excitement of competition, the thrill of the unexpected, the intricacy of the game, and the chance to admire the athletes' skills and grace under pressure, the technicalities of the final score were equally unimportant. The Mets had won, and it had been an absolutely magnificent baseball game. Even the dejected Braves players and their fans agreed on that.

But for a certain kind of sports enthusiast, the details surrounding Ventura's game-winning blow were vitally important. For the nation's sports gamblers, which team wins a game is often less important than various other arcane details—details that really have very little to do with the essence of sport or athletic competition.

One way of betting on baseball is called the over/under. In playing the over/under on a baseball game, a sports gambler wagers not on which team will win the game but on how many runs the two teams will score. The betting establishment names a figure for the total number of runs, and the gambler then bets that the two teams together will score more or less—over or under—that figure.

For the fifth game between the Mets and the Braves in the 1999 National League Championship series, the over/under was 7.5. For gamblers who had money riding on the over/under, which team actually won the game was of very little importance. What would determine whether they won or lost their bet was the total number of runs the two teams scored.

When the ball that Ventura hit cleared the outfield wall, gamblers who had bet the over were as happy as the Mets' fans at Shea Stadium. With the grand slam, the total number of runs scored went from 6 to 10, as it seemed to put the Mets ahead by a score of 7 to 3. For a moment, gamblers who had bet the over exulted, but by the next day their joy had turned to despair. When Ventura's home run was officially changed to a single, and the official final score of the game entered the record books as 4 to 3, the over bettors became losers, and the under bettors became winners. An estimated $100 million had been bet illegally with bookies around the nation on the over/under, and an equally large sum had been bet at legal sports "books" in places such as Las Vegas. In such a way does sports' "thrill of victory and agony of defeat" take on an entirely different meaning for the nation's millions of sports gamblers.

Chapter Two

The Thrill of Competition?

*J*ason was beginning to think he was in some serious trouble. He was in over his head, and he didn't know what to do about it. He had never imagined that something like this could happen to him.

Jason had loved sports for as long as he could remember. He wasn't an excellent player, but he loved to play just about anything—soccer, baseball, football, basketball, whatever was in season. When he wasn't playing, he was watching. And even more than watching, he was studying. He considered himself more a student of the games than a mere fan. A lot of kids were better athletes, but no one knew more about sports than Jason.

Jason started out with sports gambling by playing the football betting cards that some of the boys circulated at school. The cards were so common that Jason found it impossible to think of them as gambling. The guys at the fast-food restaurant where he worked also passed them around each week, and so did the people at his father's office.

The cards were very simple to play. Sometimes called parlays, each one listed all that weekend's games in the National Football League, as well as a selection of the most important contests in college football. The bettor could "play" anywhere from three to twelve games. To play, the bettor selected which team in a particular game would win against what is known as the point spread. If Jason played three games, for example, he had to pick the point-spread winner in all three. If he succeeded, the card paid off at odds of five to one, which meant that if Jason paid $5 to play that week, he would receive $25 if he won. Obviously, picking more winners was more difficult, so if Jason played twelve games and managed to get all of them right, the card would pay off at one hundred to one.

Jason figured the cards would be a cinch. For someone as well-informed as he was, he thought it would be easy to find three games—out of approximately thirty listed on the card each week—that would be surefire winners.

At first he was right. He won three out of the first four weeks that he played. The amounts that he played were small, $10 or $15 out of his weekly salary from the restaurant, but it put some extra money in his pocket, and it was good to feel like a winner.

The next weeks were not as successful, but that was okay. For four straight weeks Jason didn't win, but he was only betting a small amount, and it was still fun. It made him follow the sport even more closely, if that was possible, and the games were even more exciting to watch when he had some money riding on them.

The real trouble started when one of the seniors approached him. The other kids said that Tony Gee, as everyone referred to him, was the one who distributed all the cards around school, collected the money, and made sure the winners got paid. Tony asked Jason if he was interested in another way of betting. The parlays were for chumps, Tony Gee explained. They were sucker bets. In the long run, Tony explained, the only ones who made money on the parlays were the bookies.

"Why not bet on individual games?" Tony asked. "You're knowledgeable enough. Why not

just pick one game that you know is a sure thing, and play that one? That's the way the serious guys do it. I know a bookie; you can go through me. He can handle any action you want."

Afterward, it was hard for Jason to say exactly when the nightmare began, but it was sometime not long after he met Tony Gee. He thought it would be easy to pick winners, but every time he won, he wanted to bet again because he was feeling lucky, and every time he lost he wanted to bet again, quickly, to win his money back. And each bet was larger than the last, for similar reasons. Money for betting took a bigger chunk out of his paycheck every week, and the "research" he did for his bets took up a greater amount of his time. Football is played only one day a week, but football season led into basketball season, which led into baseball season, and there were games every night. That meant that soon Jason was betting every night.

Tony Gee was willing to give Jason credit when he did not have the money ready to cover his bets right away. At first, Jason thought this was pretty cool of Tony, but after a while he realized that Tony liked having Jason in debt to him. That way, Jason had no choice but to keep betting. How else was he going to get the money that he owed to Tony and the bookie?

People who can't pay their gambling debts often find themselves in big trouble.

The stress was unbearable. Jason felt like he was constantly wired, like he had electricity shooting through his veins. He couldn't sleep, study, or concentrate at school. All he could think about was the money he owed and his next bet. The fun of watching sports was long gone; he didn't care anymore who won or lost, just whether his teams covered the spread or beat the over/under.

One day Tony Gee took Jason out behind the school for a talk. "Do you have any idea how much you're in for?" Tony asked him, meaning did Jason know how much money he owed for his gambling. Jason had to admit that he had no idea. The truth of it was that he didn't want to know, and he was afraid to find out.

It is not unusual for people with a gambling addiction to steal from loved ones to pay back debts.

"Eighty-seven hundred dollars, pal," Tony said. "Now, we've been cool, but I can't take any more of your action until you're settled up. I need the money in a week."

Stunned by the amount Tony had named, Jason was too frightened to ask what would happen if he was not able to pay up. He had heard a lot of crazy stories, stuff about bookies having people threatened or even beaten up, and he did not want to find out if any of them were true.

The worst night of Jason's life was the night he took his parents' bank and credit cards and maxed them out for cash advances from ATM machines. He sat at the kitchen table and listened as his mother phoned her banks and *credit card companies reporting the theft. He knew that it had never entered her mind that her son was the culprit.*

Jason thought that he had been scared straight. He had done a terrible thing, but at least he was paid up with Tony. But the guilt about what he had done to his parents ate away at him. It was almost as bad as the stress he felt when he was still gambling. He promised himself that he would find a way to pay back the money he had stolen.

Then he had an idea. His sports gambling days were over, but what if he made one last bet? If he was patient and did his research, he could certainly find the surest of sure things. And now that Tony had seen that he could pay back such a large sum, he was sure to give him credit to make one bet large enough to cover the money he had stolen. Maybe, Jason thought, his little walk on the wild side of sports gambling could have a happy ending.

What Is Sports Gambling?

Sports gambling is any form of wagering or betting on the outcome of a sporting event or series of events. There are as many different varieties of such wagers as there are varieties of sporting contests. Types of sports gambling with which most people are familiar include betting on horse races and any of the professional and collegiate sports that are popular in the United States, especially football, basketball, and baseball.

The most essential difference between sports gambling and other forms of gambling is that in sports gambling the bettor is wagering on how other human beings will perform in some kind of competition or contest. The bettor himself is not part of the game, sport, or contest and cannot influence the outcome of the event.

In other kinds of gambling, the bettor has the opportunity to participate directly. Examples of this kind of gambling are the games of chance played in casinos: card games such as poker, blackjack (twenty-one), and baccarat; dice games such as craps; and slot machines. Although many people do not consider them gambling, state lotteries such as Lotto or Powerball are also examples of this kind of gambling.

Legal Vs. Illegal Gambling

In the United States today, gambling is conducted both legally and illegally. Before the 1990s, gambling was legal in only a very few locations. The largest and most well-known location was the state of Nevada, especially its glittering largest city, Las Vegas. Built in the desert, "Vegas" was developed specifically as an entertainment center and mecca for gamblers. For decades,

Las Vegas, Nevada, is the most famous gambling mecca in the world.

Nevada was virtually the only place in the United States where bettors could gamble legally in a casino setting. During that time, many Americans thought of gambling as something tawdry, disreputable, immoral, dangerous, and quite rightly illegal. The association of many of the first Vegas hotels and casinos with organized crime figures helped to sustain that image.

In the last ten years or so, this image of gambling has changed for many people. In part, this is the result of a concentrated effort by the gaming industry to make gambling more presentable. At the same time, an enormous number of states have turned to forms of legalized gambling as a means of gaining revenue for the government. The most common form that such legalized gambling has taken is lotteries administered directly by state and local governments. Today, thirty-seven states, plus the District of Columbia, Puerto Rico, and the U.S. Virgin Islands, offer some kind of state lottery. The most common kind is a variety of lotto, which is itself a variation on the old form of illegal lottery, known in many city neighborhoods as the numbers. In lotto, the player pays a small amount for a ticket on which he or she picks a series of numbers—$2, for example, to pick six numbers in New York State's Lotto. Picking all six numbers correctly guarantees a spectacular payoff, anywhere from a couple of million dollars to more than $100 million.

Lotteries have proved to be so popular that many state governments now rely on the revenue they gain from this form of legalized gambling. In the fiscal year 1998, the total sales from state lotteries in the United States was just short of $36 billion. Averaged out, that is as if every U.S. citizen spent $153 that year on lottery gambling.

With the success of the lotteries, many states started to consider other means of gaining revenue from gambling. The result was that the legislatures in several states, particularly in the South and the West, okayed certain other forms of legalized gambling.

The most common form this has taken is riverboat casinos anchored in the Mississippi River and its tributaries and along the Gulf Coast in the American South. There, gamblers are able to indulge in the usual range of casino gambling, including poker, blackjack, dice, roulette, and slot machines.

Most forms of sports gambling remain illegal everywhere outside of Nevada. Although the gaming industry is hopeful that sports gambling will become legal in more states across the country, professional and collegiate sports, which are enormously wealthy and powerful industries in their own right, are adamantly opposed to more widespread legalization. In large part, this is because the leaders of these sports fear the corrupting influence on their games that gambling has demonstrated in the past.

Horse racing and betting go hand in hand; without wagering, the sport would probably not survive.

The most common form of legal sports gambling is wagering on horse racing, which is legal at horse-racing tracks and off-site betting parlors in many states. As a sport in the United States and elsewhere, horse racing developed in association with gambling. The sport is so closely associated with betting that without wagering, it would be unable to generate sufficient spectator interest to survive as an industry.

Worth Billions

Its illegality in most places has not kept sports gambling from thriving. Across the United States in 1998, a total of more than $700 billion was wagered legally. An estimated additional $175 billion was bet illegally on various forms of sports gambling, according to the Council on Compulsive Gambling of New Jersey.

Obviously, these are enormous sums of money. This staggering total attests to the immense popularity of gambling in general and sports gambling in particular, despite the uncertain legal status of both.

For most of those who bet the sums that comprise this total, gambling is nothing more than a pastime or entertainment. Most of those who gamble, on sports or anything else, do so without ever getting into serious trouble because of it. But for a small and significant percentage of people, such as Jason, gambling is an extremely high-risk activity, one that can prove as dangerous as experimenting with alcohol and drugs. For such individuals, gambling, like alcohol or drug use, can lead to addiction.

Chapter Three | No One Beats the Spread

*T*he *world champions did not know what to make of him. Winners of the American League pennant in fourteen out of the last sixteen years, the New York Yankees thought they had seen everything there was to see on a ball field, but they had never seen anything like this. The Yankees set the standard for how you were supposed to carry yourself on the diamond, and it was not anything like what this kid was doing.*

First, there was the way the kid looked. The Yankees' image was epitomized by Mickey Mantle. Tall, blond, handsome, and muscular, Mantle in the famous Yankee pin-striped uniform was the picture of All-American baseball elegance. But this rookie in the Cincinnati Reds' uniform that Florida spring morning was something else entirely.

He did not look like a ballplayer, that was for sure. He was short and squat, built something like a fire hydrant. His face, said one of the Yankees, looked like a "clenched fist." Another put it more simply: The kid was "plug ugly." Above the rough-looking face a severe brush cut made the rookie's hair stand straight up like the bristles on a frightened porcupine.

But it was more than the way the rookie looked that annoyed the arrogant Yankees. This was a spring training game, an exhibition, and spring training was a time to take things a little easy, to work out the winter kinks in the Florida sunshine, to ease into shape for the long grind of the upcoming season. But this rookie, this "busher" as the Yankees called him, meaning that he belonged in the bush, or minor, leagues, not in major league ball with the real players, was playing as if it was the seventh game of the World Series. He was baiting the umpires, yakking away at the pitcher, jockeying the Yankees from the bench. Just who the heck does this kid think he is, the Yankees wanted to know.

When he ran the bases, the kid slid headfirst. No one had seen anything like that before. Maybe they did stuff like that down in the minors, but the kid was in the big leagues now. What a busher! What was he, some sort of show-off? The absolute worst came when, in the late innings of the slow-paced game, he worked out a walk. Instead of jogging slowly down to first, like a real big-leaguer, he sprinted as fast as he could, like a Little Leaguer in his very first game. Who was he trying to impress? What a hot dog!

Then one of the Yankees did it. "Hey, get a load of Charlie Hustle out there!" he shouted out, using the sarcastic humor characteristic of ballplayers. The Yankees in the dugout all cracked up, and the players on the field hid their faces behind their gloves to hide their laughter. Across the diamond, in the Cincinnati dugout, the Reds' players turned away so they would not be seen laughing at their new teammate. At first base, the rookie looked satisfied and oblivious.

The nickname stuck, but twenty-some years later no one was laughing at Charlie Hustle anymore. On the ball field, Pete Rose—that was the Cincinnati player's real name—had never stopped hustling or changed his style. And his headlong style of play served him well. In 1985, Rose struck his number 4,192 hit in the major leagues. With that blow, Rose broke one of baseball's longest-standing records, Ty Cobb's mark for the most hits in baseball history. That record alone certified Rose as one of baseball's all-time greats, but there was plenty of other evidence as well. Charlie Hustle had gone on to

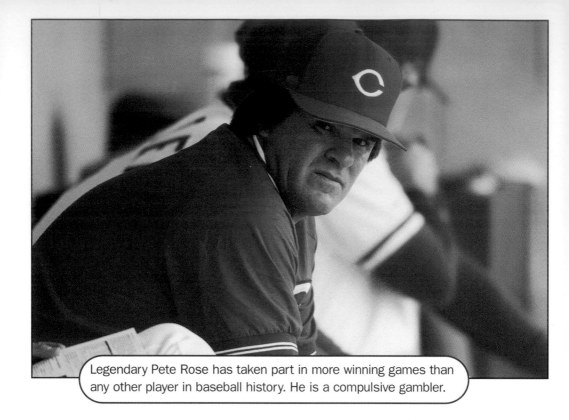
Legendary Pete Rose has taken part in more winning games than any other player in baseball history. He is a compulsive gambler.

make himself an all-star at several different positions in the infield and in the outfield, a batting champion, a National League MVP, and a star player on five World Series teams, including three world champions.

On the field, Rose's hard-nosed style made him the quintessential winner. It is believed he took part in more winning games than any other player in history. Near the end of his playing career, Rose put his mastery of baseball strategy to work as the manager of his beloved Cincinnati Reds, leading the team to several finishes high in the league standings.

Sadly, there was one honor Rose would never receive. For a major league baseball player, the ultimate accolade is to be elected to the National Baseball Hall of

Fame in Cooperstown, New York. A player is first eligible for election five years after his retirement. Only the very greatest of the great are elected to the Hall of Fame in their first year of eligibility. It seemed certain that Rose would take his place among them.

Off the field, though, Rose was into a different kind of hustle. The professionals who treat compulsive gamblers sometimes divide them into two categories: escape gamblers and action gamblers. Escape gamblers prefer slot machines, bingo, and lotteries. Basically, they use gambling to numb themselves to problems in their lives that they feel they cannot solve or face. Most suffer from depression. The majority of escape gamblers are women; many are married to men who are themselves addicted to gambling, drugs, or alcohol.

Sports gamblers generally fall into the category of action gamblers. Action gamblers tend to be male, extremely competitive, and excessively concerned with status, which they define in terms of winning and losing. Some experts even qualify individuals who speculate heavily in the stock market as a kind of action gambler. Action gamblers generally gamble for much longer before seeking treatment than escape gamblers do.

Rose was a perfect example of an action gambler. As his playing career came to an end, he replaced the action he found on the field with the action he found betting on sports.

Even while he was running the Reds from the dugout as their manager, Rose was dispatching clubhouse boys and sometimes even players to the clubhouse to talk to bookies on the phone, make bets, and track the progress of other games. Rose bet on the horses, basketball, football, and, most disturbingly, on baseball. Professional athletes in the United States are strongly discouraged from betting on sports, but they are absolutely forbidden to bet on games in their own sport.

Rose's descent into compulsive gambling cost him his job as the manager of the Reds and caused him enormous financial difficulties. His money troubles, in turn, resulted in a felony conviction for tax fraud and a prison sentence. Finally, Rose received a lifetime ban from baseball, which is why to this day the man with the most hits in the history of the game is not in the sport's Hall of Fame. Instead, with Joe Jackson, another extraordinary hitter whose career was destroyed by sports gambling, Rose now occupies a prominent place in baseball's Hall of Shame.

The House Always Wins

Obviously, the fact that sports gambling is illegal virtually everywhere in the United States does not keep millions of Americans, including teens and young adults, from engaging in it. You are probably familiar with several forms of sports gambling. The kind of football parlays or cards that Jason first got himself into trouble with are very common in schools and workplaces. You probably know someone who has participated in a Super Bowl pool or a pool for the "March Madness" of the NCAA college basketball tournament. Indeed, these two events are the sporting contests that are most heavily wagered on.

In Las Vegas and elsewhere in Nevada, sports gambling is legal. It is conducted by what is called the sports book of the casinos where other forms of legalized gambling also takes place. A book, bookmaker, or bookie is an individual or establishment that sets odds and takes bets. At the sports book at a large casino in Vegas, it is possible to bet on everything from the outcome of an individual sporting event that night to long-term wagers on which football team is likely to win next year's Super Bowl, for example.

To be successful, the book—sometimes referred to as "the house"—has to do a lot more than simply collect money from bettors and pay out to winners. A book's success depends on how well it does at setting the odds. For the most popular sports in the United States— baseball, football, and basketball—the most important way of establishing odds is through what is known as the point spread.

Basically, the point spread is the way the house ensures that it makes money from handling bets no matter which team wins the game in question. Since football is the sport on which the most money is gambled in the United States, let's use that game as an example.

In order to make money, the house first has to encourage people to bet. The house cannot make money on a game unless people bet on it. But some games are more attractive to sports gamblers than others. Consider an imaginary game between the Denver Broncos and the New Orleans Saints. In our scenario, the Broncos have won three straight Super Bowls. The Saints, meanwhile, have never even been to the play-offs in the more than thirty years they have been in the National Football League. The game is being played halfway through the regular season, in which the Broncos have won all eight of their games and the Saints have won none. In addition, the game is to be played in Denver, at the Broncos' home stadium, where it is next to impossible for a visiting team to win.

Obviously, the Broncos would have to be considered overwhelming favorites to win this particular game. Most gamblers—perhaps almost all—could be expected to bet on the Broncos. There would be no good reason for them not to.

In these circumstances, however, there would be little reason for the house to take such bets. Think about it: Suppose a total of $1,000 is bet at the casino on the game. This figure is called the take. Nine hundred dollars of it is bet on the Broncos, $100 on the Saints. The house has thus, in effect, bet $800 on the Saints. If the Broncos win, the house is down $800 ($900 in payout to the winning gamblers minus $100 in losing bets on the Saints).

Obviously, the house is not going to be in business long if it makes bets like that. The house does not want to be making bets at all because the house knows that in the end all bettors lose. Instead, what the house does is to make it more attractive to bet on the Saints. The goal is to ensure that the take is balanced as closely as possible between both sides of the bet. In other words, to take in $500 on the Broncos and $500 on the Saints, so that no matter which team wins, the house is not out any money. How would the house make money then? By charging each bettor a fee to handle their bet. This fee or sum is sometimes called the vigorish, or the vig for short. The reason the house always wins is because it makes its money on the vig and not by betting.

The Line

So how does the house make each game attractive to bettors and ensure that the take is evenly distributed? By setting what is called the point spread, or the line. For example, in the Broncos-Saints game, the book would essentially "give" the Saints a certain number of points to begin the game. In this case, let's say the house establishes the Broncos as 16-point favorites. Sixteen points is the line, or the point spread.

Kids sometimes give one another "lead" points in games if one player is significantly better.

Essentially, for the purposes of sports gamblers, the Saints have been given a sixteen-point lead, just as kids playing in the schoolyard might give the weaker team or player a lead of a certain number of points. The person who bets on the Saints is said to take the points; the person who bets on the Broncos is said to give the points. The spread does not affect the actual score of the game, but only the "score" so far as bettors are concerned. For the bettor on the Broncos to win, Denver must beat New Orleans by more than sixteen points. A bettor on the Saints wins if New Orleans wins the game or if the Saints lose by less than sixteen points.

In this way, the point spread works to make betting on the Saints a much more attractive proposition for sports gamblers. Many people think that the line or spread is an expert assessment of the strengths and weaknesses of the two teams in question. It is, to a certain extent, but not totally. The line is equally a kind of assessment of the loyalties of bettors. In the time leading up to the game, the line can move. If too many bettors take the Saints, then the spread will come down until Denver becomes more attractive to gamblers, and so on.

Some form of the line or spread is the most common way of gambling on baseball, football, and basketball. That's why sports gamblers do not talk about which team won or lost the game but about whether the team they bet on "covered" or "beat" the spread. Imagine that Denver beats New Orleans 30 to 20. In that case, sports gamblers who took the Saints win their bet because New Orleans covered the spread, even though it lost the game. Likewise, although Denver won the game, those who bet on the Broncos lost because the Broncos did not cover.

These days, sports gambling is so widespread in the United States that the point spread is published in the sports sections of most newspapers, right alongside the standings, statistics, and box scores. Many papers employ columnists to advise readers as to which are the best bets to make. Many sports sections also carry advertising from tout services, which sell such advice for a fee.

Other forms of sports gambling include over/under bets. Horse racing and boxing use an odds system to

The Internet provides bettors with easy and instant access to point spreads and other gambling information.

ensure that the house is protected. A professional handicapper assigns each horse in a race odds against its
winning. A horse goes "off," as gamblers say, at 2 to 1,
or 5 to 1, for example. If the horse wins, the house pays
the gambler the amount he or she bet times the odds.
Like the line or spread, the odds change depending on
how the take is distributed among the bets on all the
horses in the race. In a prizefight, the house assigns the
boxer considered less likely to win odds against him
beating the favorite. In the days leading up to the fight,
these odds can change depending on how much money
is being wagered on which fighter.

Illegal sports gambling works the same way. Bookies
usually use the line or odds established by the sports
books, which are available in the newspapers. These
odds are offered to their clients. In some cases, a
bookie's odds may vary, especially when the bookie is
taking action on a local team. Bookies may also charge
more vigorish for handling bets than a legal sports
book would.

Increased access to the Internet has contributed a
great deal to the rise in sports gambling in the United
States over the last ten years or so. A very simple
search on the Internet instantly turns up literally hun-
dreds of sites devoted to providing information on
point spreads and allowing bettors to gamble illegally
on sports on-line.

Chapter Four

Danger Signs

*A*t sixteen, Art Schlichter was already a
golden boy in the football-crazy state of Ohio. As
the star quarterback of one of the state's best
high school teams, at seventeen Schlichter was
one of the most heavily recruited players in the
country by the nation's college football powers.
When at eighteen he decided to stay "home"
and play for Ohio State, it seemed like the whole
state rejoiced.

At nineteen, Schlichter started as quarterback
for the highly ranked Ohio State Buckeyes, the
first player in the history of the school to do so.
At twenty, Schlichter was on the cover of Sports
Illustrated, *and Ohio State went through its
regular season undefeated. The clean-cut,*

soft-spoken Schlichter was the most popular athlete in the state. At the age of twenty-one, his biography, Straight Arrow, was published.

At twenty-two, Schlichter finished his college career. He was taken in the first round of the NFL draft by the Baltimore Colts and signed a contract that made him a wealthy young man. Everyone predicted great things for him.

By twenty-four, Schlichter himself says, "I was a horrible player. I couldn't concentrate. It was as if I'd lost all my skills. Emotionally, I was shot." Gone, too, was every penny of the $350,000 signing bonus the Colts had given him, all of it gambled away on sports. At age twenty-five, Schlichter, who was making $140,000 a year, lost $300,000 betting on sports in just one week. Gone soon would be his career, as the NFL suspended him for betting on its own games.

At twenty-six, Schlichter was reinstated in the NFL after receiving treatment for compulsive gambling. At twenty-eight, he was suspended again, this time permanently, for sports gambling. He continued to gamble. At thirty-one, he was arrested for writing a bad check. By the time he was thirty-three, he was stealing money from his own wife.

At thirty-four, Schlichter was serving a sentence in a federal penitentiary in Terre Haute,

Indiana. He had been convicted of bank fraud for writing $175,000 in worthless checks to feed his gambling addiction. His wife had left him. Upon completion of his sentence, he can anticipate being charged with additional felonies for other frauds he committed.

Problem Gambling

Art Schlichter is a compulsive gambler, which is one of many terms used for individuals for whom gambling has become an addiction and a disease. Other common terms used are problem gambling and pathological gambling. These terms are often used interchangeably. Some people, however, distinguish between them, with problem gambling being used as a catchall phrase for the various stages along the way to gambling addiction.

Gambling addiction is generally recognized as a disease. Both the American Psychiatric Association and the World Health Organization recognize it as such. For the gambling addict, the disease progresses from disrupting his or her life to taking it over as the bettor loses control over all aspects of his or her gambling, including when, where, and how much to gamble.

In its progression and consequences, gambling addiction has many elements in common with other addictions, especially alcoholism or drug addiction. In fact, gambling addicts are often "cross-addicted" to alcohol or drugs as well.

Like those diseases, gambling addiction grows worse over time if it is not treated. For the gambling addict, gambling causes changes in the body's chemistry and nervous system, which is why the gambler at first experiences pleasurable sensations when gambling. Like other kinds of addicts, the pathological gambler experiences unpleasurable physical and emotional sensations—withdrawal symptoms—when he or she attempts to stop. Similarly, the gambling addict has to increase his or her level of involvement with gambling to achieve the same level of excitement or pleasure. Experts refer to this as tolerance.

Symptoms

The Diagnostic and Statistical Manual of Mental Disorders, Fourth Edition (DSM-IV) is the official diagnostic handbook of the American Psychiatric Association. According to the *DSM-IV*, a pathological gambler exhibits at least five of the following behaviors:

- Preoccupation with gambling

- Needs to gamble with increasing amounts of money to achieve the desired effect

A preoccupation with gambling is one symptom of a pathological gambler.

- Repeated unsuccessful efforts to cut back, control, or stop gambling

- Restlessness or irritability when attempting to control or stop gambling

- Gambling as a way of escaping from problems or relieving unpleasant feelings

- "Chasing" losses—following big losses by gambling even larger sums to get even

- Lies to family members, therapists, or others to conceal the extent of gambling

- Commits illegal acts—fraud, theft, forgery, or embezzlement—to finance gambling

- Suffers negative consequences at work or in an important relationship because of gambling

- Relies on others to relieve financial troubles caused by gambling

The official medical definition of pathological gambling, as established by psychiatrist Richard Rosenthal, is a "progressive disease or disorder characterized by a continuous or periodic loss of control over gambling; a preoccupation with gambling and with obtaining money with which to gamble; irrational thinking; and a continuation of the behavior despite adverse consequences."

Who Is at Risk?

Pathological gamblers are more likely to be:

- ◆ Male

- ◆ Children of pathological gamblers

- ◆ People with the attitude that money is the cause and solution of all problems

- ◆ People with a lower-than-average level of income

- ◆ Unmarried or not involved in a meaningful relationship

How Common Is It?

Two-thirds of pathological gamblers are male. On average, males begin gambling earlier, usually in adolescence. Females tend to be more resistant to seeking treatment for problem gambling. In general, female gamblers tend to be the more passive or escape type of gambler.

The best estimates indicate that 1 to 5 percent of the entire population are problem gamblers. It is also estimated that 1 to 3 percent of the population would meet the criteria for pathological gambling. For some people, gambling addiction can begin with their very first bet. More commonly, the disease progresses over many years, with the gambler able to first maintain a level of

Compulsive gambling is a mostly male problem, usually beginning in adolescence.

social gambling. Often a period of stress or depression triggers the urge to gamble.

Sports gamblers differ in some significant ways from the typical problem gambler. Sports gamblers are even more likely to be male than the average gambler. They also tend to be better educated and more successful economically than the average gambler.

Teen Gamblers

As with other addictions, teens tend to be at higher risk for pathological gambling than adults. The National Institutes of Mental Health estimates that 7 to 11 percent of teenagers are pathological gamblers. Why teens should be at higher risk for addiction to gambling is uncertain. Medical experts speculate that, as with other addictions, teens may be more vulnerable because they have not yet fully developed physically, emotionally, and psychologically.

Although the gaming industry denies it vigorously, evidence indicates that the increased exposure to gambling that has resulted from its more widespread legalization has resulted in an increase in problem gambling. Those places where gambling has recently been legalized have also experienced a rise in the negative consequences associated with problem gambling, including depression, suicide, severe legal and financial troubles, and increases in the rates of divorce and domestic violence. Mental health professionals believe that legalization does lead to an increase in compulsive gambling. The *DSM-IV* also asserts that the onset of pathological gambling can result from exposure to legalized gambling.

Obviously, these trends have enormous consequences for teens. If the trend of increased acceptance of gambling continues, it can be expected that the rate of problem gambling among teens will also continue to rise. Teen gambling in all forms, including betting on sports, has risen steadily since the 1980s. In a recent survey, one-third of teens questioned indicated that they had gambled for money at least once before reaching the age of eleven. Over 80 percent said that by the age of fifteen they had gambled either legally or illegally.

Indicators

Physicians and therapists refer to gambling addiction as an insidious disease, which means that its progress is difficult to detect until the person has lost control over his or her gambling. Even at that point, the gambler is usually the last person to recognize or admit the degree to which the disease has taken over. Gamblers Anonymous is an organization devoted to enabling problem gamblers to find a way to help themselves. Together with the California Council on Problem Gambling, it has compiled a list of indicators to help teens and those who care about them determine whether they are developing a problem with gambling. These warning signs include:

- Unexplained absences from school or classes
- Sudden drop in grades or other signs of decreased performance at school
- Change in personality or behavior
- Exaggerated display of money or new material possessions
- Participation in daily or weekly card games for money
- Bragging about winning at gambling
- Intense interest in gambling conversations

Exaggerated display of new material possessions can be a warning sign of a gambling addiction.

- Unusual interest in any sources of information about sports

- Unlikely explanations when asked about obtaining new possessions or the whereabouts of old ones

- Borrowing or stealing money

- Unreasonable or unlikely explanations for "losing" valuable gifts given to them, for example, at birthdays or Christmas

- Increased social isolation, especially withdrawal from family or friends

- Exaggerated use of gambling terms in conversation

Getting Help

Gambling addiction is not a disease that gets better on its own. If you suspect that you or someone you know has a problem with sports gambling or with any form of gambling, you need to reach out for help. The best place to start is with a local chapter of Gamblers Anonymous, which can provide you with the information and assistance you need. Most states where gambling has been legalized also have public, nonprofit organizations that provide information and help to people who experience problems because of gambling. The National Council on Problem Gambling is also a

Public, nonprofit organizations can provide information to people who experience problems because of gambling.

good resource. Some of these organizations are listed in the back of this book; others can be contacted through Gamblers Anonymous or found in your local phone book. At the very least, talk to someone you trust—a parent, relative, teacher, or friend. Be as honest as you can be about the situation and about the fact that you are asking for help.

Not Such a Long Shot

The same factors that put teens at increased risk for problem gambling also mean that teens have a greater chance for successful treatment, provided that the problem is recognized and treated early enough. Experts estimate that self-help programs such as

Gamblers Anonymous, when combined with other treatment, such as therapy or counseling, result in a success rate of more than 50 percent. Therapy is especially important because people often turn to gambling as a way of "managing" other stressful issues in their life, such as unhappiness at home, job troubles, difficulty with relationships, and so on. In the long run, treatment for problem gambling is unlikely to be successful unless these issues are addressed as well. In addition, the disease of pathological gambling can create other enormous problems for the gambler, including emotional difficulties, such as depression; ruined marriages, friendships, and other relationships; and legal and financial difficulties. These problems remain even after the person has decided to get treatment for gambling addiction.

Chapter Five

Say It Ain't So

*I*t is one of the most famous baseball legends, and quite possibly the saddest. On a summer day in 1920, Joe Jackson left the office of the new baseball commissioner, Judge Kenesaw Mountain Landis. An outfielder for the Chicago White Sox, Jackson was one of the greatest baseball players anyone had ever seen. An excellent left-handed hitter, Jackson was powerful at the plate and fast in the field and on the bases. Over thirteen major league seasons, Jackson had compiled a .356 life-time batting average, which to this day remains the second-highest in baseball history. He led the league in triples eight times, regularly ranked among the league leaders in batting average and extra-base hits, and even hit over .400 in one season. Of Jackson in the field, it was said that his glove was "where triples went to die."

His skills made Jackson the best all-around player on what many considered to be the best team in the game, the Chicago White Sox. He was also one of the most popular. Born poor in rural Pickens County, South Carolina, Jackson had received very little education. He was nicknamed "Shoeless" Joe Jackson because, the story went, when growing up he had always been too poor to afford a real pair of baseball shoes. When, as a minor leaguer, he received his first pair of spikes, he was at first so unused to them that he preferred to play in his socks. His humble beginnings and gentle, unsophisticated nature made him a favorite of fans, particularly kids.

All during that season of 1920, rumors swirled around the White Sox. The team had unexpectedly been beaten in the 1919 World Series, and sportswriters and fans insisted that there had been something funny about the games. An investigation revealed that eight White Sox players had either been approached by gamblers about "throwing"—intentionally losing—the series, had actually taken money, or knew about the scheme and had not reported their teammates. In the late summer of 1920, the eight players were indicted by a grand jury for conspiring to *throw the World Series. Soon afterward, they were called in to meet with Commissioner Landis, who told them they were banned from professional baseball forever.*

As the story goes, a group of kids, some of Jackson's young fans, were waiting outside when Jackson left the building where the meeting had been held. In teary-eyed disbelief, they begged Jackson to tell them that the bad news was not true. "Say it ain't so, Joe," they begged, sniffling, over and over again, holding on to the player's legs as he walked slowly away. "I'm afraid it is, fellas," Jackson said, brokenhearted himself.

Jason's story had a happier ending. He was all set to make his "last bet," to win back the money he had stolen from his parents. But something—he couldn't say what it was—stopped him. Instead, he talked about his situation with a teacher at school, who told him how to go about getting help. Several days later, Jason attended a meeting of Gamblers Anonymous that was held in the basement of a local church. After a few minutes, he heard the man who was running the meeting announce that there was a new person attending that evening. Jason knew that this was his chance. "Hello," he said quietly as he stood up. "My name is Jason, and I have a problem with gambling."

A Gamblers Anonymous meeting is a good place to seek help for a gambling problem.

Glossary

action gambler A gambler who bets primarily for the feelings of excitement and heightened awareness that betting gives him or her; most sports gamblers are action gamblers.

bookmaker A person who sets odds and takes bets.

casino A building devoted to gambling.

compulsive gambling Term often used as a synonym for pathological gambling.

escape gambler A gambler who bets primarily as a way to numb himself and escape from other problems in life.

favorite The team or competitor considered most likely to win an athletic event.

fix An attempt by gamblers to prearrange the outcome of a sporting event.

handicapper A person who establishes the odds for betting on a sporting event, especially on horse racing; also, a person who bets on horses.

house A person or establishment that takes bets or establishes odds.

legalized gambling Forms of gambling permitted under the law. In the United States the most common form of legalized gambling is state lotteries.

line   The odds established for betting on a sporting event; see also point spread.

lottery   Form of gambling in which, most commonly, the bettor wins by correctly guessing the numbers that are drawn by the house at random.

odds   The likelihood of a competitor winning in an athletic event; also, the payoff for a winning bet on that competitor.

over/under   Type of wager on a sporting event in which the gambler bets on the total number of runs or points scored.

pathological gambling   Preferred medical term for the disease of gambling addiction.

point spread   Advantage in runs or points given to a team for the purpose of sports gambling.

problem gambling   Term used for gambling that is causing problems in an individual's life or is threatening to grow out of control; generally used to refer to gambling that is less severe than compulsive or pathological gambling.

sports book   Part of a casino devoted to various forms of sports gambling.

sports gambling   Betting on an athletic contest.

throw   To intentionally lose a game or manipulate its outcome, usually for the purpose of affecting gambling on the event.

tolerance   Process of building up a reduced effect to an addictive substance or behavior.

underdog   Team or competitor considered least likely to win an athletic event.

vigorish   Term used by some gamblers or bookmakers to refer to the fee charged for taking a bet.

withdrawal   Unpleasant symptoms resulting from attempts to stop using addictive substances or to change addictive behavior.

For Further Reading

Dolan, Edward F. *Teenagers and Compulsive Gambling.* Danbury, CT: Franklin Watts, 1994.

Haddock, Patricia. *Teens and Gambling: Who Wins?* Springfield, NJ: Enslow, 1996.

Hautman, Pete, and Owen Smith. *Stone Cold.* New York: Simon and Schuster, 1998.

Horvath, A. Thomas, and Reid K. Hester. *Sex, Drugs, Gambling, and Chocolate: A Workbook for Overcoming Addictions.* San Luis Obispo, CA: Impact, 1998.

O'Brien, Timothy L. *Bad Bet: The Inside Story of the Glamour, Glitz, and Danger of America's Gambling Industry.* New York: Times Books, 1998.

Saunders, Carol Silverman. *Straight Talk About Teenage Gambling.* New York: Facts on File, 1999.

Williams, Mary E. *Legalized Gambling.* San Diego, CA: Greenhaven, 1999.

Where to Go for Help

In the United States

Council on Compulsive Gambling of New Jersey
1315 West Street, Suite One
Trenton, NJ 08618
(609) 599-3299
(800) GAMBLER
e-mail: ccgnj@800gambler.org
Web site: http://www.800gambler.org
The council's help line can be accessed by callers in New Jersey, Kentucky, Pennsylvania, Illinois, Texas, Alaska, Mississippi, California, Nevada, and New Mexico. Callers from any other state who need help with a gambling problem should call (800) 522-4700 for immediate assistance.

Gamblers Anonymous
International Service Office
P.O. Box 17173
Los Angeles, CA 90017
(213) 386-8789
e-mail: isomain@gamblersanonymous.org
Web site: http://www.gamblersanonymous.org

National Council on Problem Gambling
208 G Street NE
Washington, DC 20002
(202) 547-9204
(800) 522-4700
e-mail: ncpg@erols.com
Web site: http://www.ncpgambling.org
Provides a complete list of individual mailing addresses, telephone numbers, e-mail addresses, and Web sites for the almost forty states that have a Council on Problem or Compulsive Gambling.

In Canada

Canadian Foundation on Compulsive Gambling
505 Consumers Road, Suite 801
Willowdale, ON N2J 4V8
(416) 499-8260
(416) 499-9800
e-mail: cf@ncpgambling.org
Web site: http://www.cfcg.on.ca

Index

About the Author

Joshua D. G. Willker is a writer, teacher, and adventurer. He is currently conducting an experiment in unassisted wilderness living in the Great Woods of the American Northeast.

Photo Credits

Cover and interior shots by Bob Van Lindt except pp. 7 © Ezra Shaw/Allsport; pp. 10, 22 © Al Bello/Allsport; p. 25 © Matthew Stockman/Allsport; p. 30 © Jim Commentucci/Allsport and p. 52 © Rick Brady/Uniphoto.

Layout

Geri Giordano